THE IDLER GUIDE TO C

THE IDLER GUIDE TO

CLASSICAL MUSIC

Sandy Burnett

IDLER PRESS

MMXV

Published by Idler Press

81 WESTBOURNE PARK ROAD   LONDON   W2 5QH

ISBN 978-0-9548456-7-4

Pattern design by Alice Smith

Typesetting by Bracketpress

Second Edition

www.idler.co.uk

Contents

Introduction   1

1. The Baroque Era (1607–1759)   3

2. The Classical Era (1760–1805)   15

3. The Romantic era (1805–1910)   23

4. Terrific Uproar: a violent interlude (1913)   32

5. The Last Hundred Years (1915–2015)   40

Introduction

This is an introduction to classical music, which covers four consecutive historical periods: Baroque, Classical, Romantic, and The Last Hundred Years, as well as A Violent Interlude which took place in 1913. Each chapter begins with an overview of an era, then examines one piece of music in detail. This is a book to make classical music accessible, but unlike some other guides it doesn't shy away from technical terms. On the contrary, I want to give people the tools to go to an opera, concert, flick through a programme booklet and understand what's going on. So the end of each chapter has a summary of the essential elements of each era, together with five useful musical terms to know.

The works examined in detail are as follows:

Johann Sebastian Bach (1685–1750):
Prelude in C major BWV846
from the Well-Tempered Klavier Book 1

Wolfgang Amadeus Mozart (1759–91):
String Quartet in B flat K458, "the Hunt"

Gustav Mahler (1860–1911): Symphony no. 1

Igor Stravinsky (1882–1971):
Le Sacre du printemps / The Rite of Spring

Steve Reich (b.1936):
Different Trains

You can buy the recordings from the usual sources, or listen to them online; you can find a playlist featuring all of the music and recordings discussed in this book here: www.sandyburnett.com/ playlists. Other recordings of the featured works can also be used in conjunction with this book – the timings indicated in the text (and occasionally the track titles) will vary, but not by much.

This book is part of Classic Discovery, a project that makes classical music accessible through talks, interactive concerts, demonstrations and workshops. Go to www.classicdiscovery.com for more information.

The Baroque Era
(1607–1759)

Half way through the eighteenth century, the French writer and politician Charles de Brosses found himself in Rome. He was a seasoned traveller, knowledgeable about many arts, and a great admirer of all things Italian, but one recently constructed building he came across in Rome – the Pamphili Palace – pleased him not. The ornamentation on its architecture was simply too fussy, with a kind of elaborate filigree which was better suited to silverware than to buildings.

De Brosses records his feelings in a letter, and the word he uses to describe this crime against architectural good taste was "baroque" – a French version of a term originally found in Portuguese to describe a misshapen pearl – uma pérola barroca. It is one of the first uses of this term, and De Brosses didn't mean it as a compliment. Since then though, the image of the misshapen pearl has been widely adopted to describe not just one extravagant architectural detail, but an entire century and a half of artistic endeavour: art, architecture, dance and music; its beauty and also its wildness; its desire to break rules and step outside the norm in order to be direct, vivid, and above all, dramatic. Listen to the first minute of any opera aria by George Friderick Handel (1685–1759) and you'll hear what I mean.

So when did this new way of thinking first take hold? A gradual transition was taking place around the year 1600, but I've taken

1607 as the starting point here, because that's the year that Claudio Monteverdi's Orfeo was first performed. A retelling of the Orpheus and Euridice myth bringing together music, poetry, dance, stage machines and "noble scenery", it was the first great example of a new genre called opera, and one that caused a lot of interest and comment for the way it had the capacity to stir the passions of those in the audience. Hitherto, in the Renaissance era, music was meant to be beautiful, easy to understand, and any dissonances or musical rough edges had to be smoothed over in the next beat. Baroque music has quite a different musical aesthetic; it set out to excite the emotions, even if it means breaking the rules of music now and again. In the prologue to Orfeo, the allegorical figure of La Musica puts it best: "I am Music," she sings, "who can soothe all troubled hearts with sweet notes, and inflame the coldest minds with noble anger and with love."

Baroque musicians in Northern Italy were perfectly placed to make the most of advances in the design of new instruments, because the world centre for violin making was right on their doorstep. In Cremona, violins, violas and cellos were being crafted by makers whose names have become legendary, none more so than Antonio Stradivarius (1644–1737), who brought his instruments to perfection thanks to perfect proportions and first-class craftsmanship. Hand in hand with the excellence of these new stringed instruments went dazzling new music that was designed to show them off. Just a day's travel from Cremona took you to Venice, where Antonio Vivaldi (1678–1741) wrote music that showed off their capabilities. His output includes over five hundred concertos, with violins starring in most of them – a concerto being a piece of music where several instruments play together ("in concert"), with regular spots for one or more soloists. The texture of the music sets out to raise the pulse-rate, with elaborate runs and striking contrasts between music that's

Louis XIV as Apollo in Le Ballet Royal de la nuit, by Henri Gissey

loud (forte) and soft (piano), quick (allegro) and at a walking pace (andante).

The focus of French music was somewhat different; elegance and grace are the watchwords here, and everything was centred around the staggeringly opulent court at Versailles greatly expanded by the "Sun King" Louis XIV. He used music to entertain, impress and intimidate both his own aristocracy and visiting dignitaries from abroad. And to dance to: he was a skilful dancer who often appeared in his own entertainments. In the Ballet royal de la nuit of 1653, Louis made an unforgettable appearance as Apollo, the Sun God, with a dazzling costume to match. And when we listen today to music of the French Baroque, by composers such as Lully (1632–87) or Rameau (1683–1764), it's the elegance of the phrasing and the delicacy of the trills, or agréments, which set the music apart as recognisably French.

Meanwhile amongst the aristocracy of Georgian England, there was a mania for Italian opera, an art form which was outlandish, ruinously expensive, and in a foreign language almost nobody could understand. Headed by George Frideric Handel – born in Northern Germany, and a master of the Italian style – London was treated to a succession of operatic entertainments, thirty-five from Handel's pen alone. Each of them was stunningly staged, and boasted the greatest and most expensive performers of the day. The star soprano Francesca Cuzzoni for example: the composer and flautist Johann Joachim Quantz (1697–1773) described her singing as "innocent and affecting," while her ornaments "took possession of the soul of every auditor." Her fee was enormous – Handel guaranteed her two thousand pounds for her first London season – and London audiences were suitably impressed. At her first performance on the twelfth of January 1723 she sang so beautifully that a footman shouted from the gallery: "Damme, she has a nest of nightingales in her belly!"

By this stage, music had moved very much to the forefront of opera. We might take that as a given these days, but what had started out in Monteverdi's day as a balanced mix of many art forms had given way to one in which music predominated. One vivid aria followed another, describing anything from love and sorrow to war, rage, and impossible moral dilemmas. These were dramatic situations in primary colours, in which operatic soloists dazzled audiences with the brilliance and freedom of their singing. So excitement, brilliance, elegance and even garishness – these are all essential elements of the Baroque mix.

It is best exemplified in the music of Johann Sebastian Bach (1685–1750). Unlike his exact contemporary Handel who left for Italy and then England in his early twenties, Bach spent all of his life in Northern Germany, in a succession of respectable if not stellar jobs for court or church. Director of music at court in Weimar and Cöthen for much of his thirties, he made his final move to Leipzig in 1723 to organise music for the city's main churches, and to teach singing to the boys of the Thomasschule there. He may not have had the dazzling career in his own lifetime that Handel enjoyed, and after his death his music almost disappeared from the public consciousness. But when Bach's music did re-emerge in the nineteenth century, it secured a central place in the history books which it has retained ever since.

Bach produced his Well-Tempered Klavier Book 1 in 1722. It was aimed at both students and fully-fledged performers – or as Bach wrote on the title page of his autograph manuscript, "for the profit and use of the musical youth desirous of learning, as well as for the pastime of those already skilled in this study." It stands as a reminder that although we might revere Bach today as one of the greatest classical composers in history, teaching was one of his main activities for the last twenty-seven years of his life. For students who were just starting out, he used to give them the Preludes and Fugues of this very volume to work on rather than dry technical exercises; he regarded them as an essential part of his teaching method, and he put together a second volume of the Well-Tempered Klavier two decades later. The fact that these prelude and fugues succeed both as student studies and master-pieces in their own right is a mark of their greatness.

I used the word masterpieces there to show how Bach can achieve so much with so little, and also to show how Bach uses restriction to create something amazingly inventive. Let's take a close look at the first work in this collection: the C major prelude BWV 846.

A prelude is a short piece of music, designed to come before something else – either another movement, or a succession of more short pieces. It could take any form. It could be like an improvisation, moving freely from one idea to another; it could be a two-sided conversation between right and left hands, exchanging ideas and building a musical argument; or it could take one short musical motif and use it as the seed out of which the entire piece grows. That last approach is the one that Bach takes in this case.

Prélude

BWV 846

J.S. Bach

RL015

Take a look at the sheet music, or indeed Bach's original autograph manuscript; a copy of either is easily accessible online. Even if you think you can't read music, you will be able to get a sense of the piece. Reading music is similar to reading a book – the eye moves from left to right, with the parts for different instruments (or for

the left and right hands of the keyboard) laid out on top of each other.

The first thing to strike you is the fact that Bach only gives us a limited amount of information on the page. There are the notes, for sure, and we'll come to them later. And we have the title – Prélude, Prelude I, or Praeludium in the original. But as for basic questions such as: how fast to play the music, how loud or soft, whether to slow down at the end, whether to accent some notes more than others – Bach gives us no clue. On one level that's frustrating. But that lack of direction is also liberating, and one of the things that makes Baroque music so satisfying to play. Why so? Because while scores by later composers – I'm thinking of Richard Strauss (1864–1949) or Igor Stravinsky (1882–1971) here – are heavily marked up with playing directions, here Bach leaves us to make up our own mind. To get the best out of Baroque music as a performer, you have to draw on your own musical instincts. And in doing so, it makes you much more engaged with the music. It's not a case of following comprehensive instructions on the page; how to shape the music and balance the individual notes on the page is entirely down to you.

Secondly, you'll probably be struck by the musical patterns on the paper. Each bar – in other words, a regular number of beats (in this case, four) divided by vertical lines – contains the same shape of notes. The pitches on the stave vary, but the pattern remains the same. To me, parallels from some of the other arts suggest themselves: perhaps the regular splashings of paint on a Jackson Pollock canvas, or the fixed intervals in which pillars occur in a Gothic cathedral. Because the content of each bar (with the exception of the last line of music) is exactly the same: a sustained bass note, followed by a spread-out version of a chord above it, following exactly the same pattern each time. A chord spread out in this way is called an arpeggio. What is striking about this piece is what is left out. There's no melody as such; and because each of the notes falls in a regular pattern, there isn't even any rhythm – since the distance of timings between the notes never varies. So at a stroke, Bach deliberately removes two of the three main musical characteristics from his piece altogether – leaving just one: harmony, the way notes are combined with each other to form chords.

That harmony unfolds, to the accompaniment of a regular pulse, throughout the piece from beginning to end. And since harmony is thrust into the spotlight in a work like this, Bach allows us to see clearly how he's using harmony as a structural device, taking us on a journey through a varied musical terrain. All we have to focus on in a piece like this is the harmonic landscape we're led through – away from our starting point and back again.

In music like this, a piece like this is in a key; in this case the key is C major. Bach states it clearly in the shape of the opening phrase and in the very last one as well; this is the home key, our point of departure and our point of return. Having a home key is the fundamental principle of the tonal system which held sway from well before Bach's time right through to the early twentieth century. The home key is known as the tonic, and the other chords within a tonal system are all relative to it, some more important than others. The sense of musical travel in this piece stems from the harmony leaving this home key and returning to it over the course of two pages. We even get a version of that journey in miniature in the first twelve seconds or so. The first bar, or pattern, is a harmonious C major; the second bar introduces a clash in its bottom two notes, with a chord of D minor over the bass note C which has been held over; the clash is resolved in the third bar, which introduces the chord of G with B in the bass – this is the so-called dominant chord in the tonal system, five steps away in the scale from the home key; and Bach brings the chord of C back in the fourth bar. So the music has gone full circle in that short space of time – from consonance to clashing dissonance, resolution and back again. This though is only the beginning of the musical journey; Bach takes the music down and up again through a number of different key areas, with each bar still inhabiting the shape of the opening bar. This continuous use of the same pattern could become repetitive; it is only the skilfully-led journey through the harmony that keeps it interesting. Towards the end of the prelude, and while the upper notes in the pattern continue to move, we become aware of a fixed bass note that continues to sound on the same pitch, rather like the tolling of a bell. You'll hear this from 1'13" in my featured recording. This is a compositional device called a pedal point, and in this case it's a dominant pedal. It serves two purposes; it anchors the music on the dominant area of the tonality; and it creates an increasing sense of tension by dropping anchor while the harmony continues to circulate above – a kind of tension which can only be released when the music resolves to the tonic once more. And it is at this point, for the first time in the piece, that Bach allows himself to break free from the pattern he's established since the very first bar, and allows a more decorative figure to bring the piece to an end.

This prelude is a piece which is marked by restrictions; Bach limits himself severely by taking melody and rhythm out of the mix, then sees what can be achieved within those narrow self-imposed boundaries. That the prelude succeeds so brilliantly, and with the minimum of apparent effort, goes to show what a remarkable composer Bach was.

But for Bach, that was just one way of doing things. Remarkably for its time, the Well-Tempered Klavier presents preludes in every single one of the major and minor keys that are possible on the keyboard: twenty-four in all. None of the other preludes in the Well-Tempered Klavier has such a relentless focus on harmony; in each of the others, Bach takes a different approach. The D major prelude for example is a right-hand workout for the keyboard player; the one in B flat is a flashy virtuosic showpiece which sounds like a written-down improvisation. And paired with each of these preludes is a fugue, a kind of piece that's completely based on imitation: a theme is stated on its own at the start, before appearing successively in all of the other parts of the contrapuntal structure, with the fingers of the keyboard player conjuring up individual voices in a choir. With the fugues too, each of them follows a different pattern: sometimes dense, sometimes playful, and written for two, three, four or five voices. Bach prided himself on exploring all of the possibilities of a given form in the most complete way possible. Being consistently inventive, pushing the technique of players to the limit, and working wonders with limited means – just some of the features that make this remarkable collection of preludes and fugues one of the most important classical works of all.

So I return to the subject of craftsmanship, which is an especially important aspect of music from the Baroque era. If you wrote music in those days, it wasn't to express your own feelings, or tell your own life story. It was to create something skilfully, and to the best of your ability. The idea of being a creative genius simply had not been invented yet. As Bach himself said, "I have had to work hard. Anyone who works as hard as me will go just as far as I have done." Bach was proud to come from a long line of composing craftsmen; musicians like him wrote music not for their own artistic desire or self-expression, but for the glory of God. And while he wrote music on a much larger scale – notably the three imposing masterpieces, the St Matthew Passion, the St John Passion, and the Mass in B minor – the essence of his music is contained in this tiny C major prelude.

a dance-like feel
rhythmic drive, led by harmony
extremes of expression
flamboyant theatricality
craftsmanship rather than self-expression

Five terms to know:

concerto: a piece of music where several instruments play together ("in concert"), with one or more instruments stepping out to take the limelight at regular intervals.

bars: regular units of musical time, usually containing two, three, or four beats, divided on the page by vertical lines. Useful for navigation purposes, like miniature mile posts.

prelude: a self-contained instrumental piece that's designed to go before something; a self-contained miniature.

tonic and dominant: the two most important key relationships in tonal music. The tonic is the home key, and the dominant is its closest relative, situated on the fifth degree of the scale.

pedal point: a device used towards the end of a piece when a note is held to anchor the harmony. Usually in the bass, and usually on the dominant.

The Classical Era
(1760–1805)

In May 1737 an unsigned letter appeared in the pages of *Der Critische Musikus*, or the Critical Musician, a Hamburg-based journal aimed at general music lovers. Without actually naming him, Johann Sebastian Bach was the subject of a long and bitter attack. "This great man," it argued, "would be the admiration of whole nations if he had more amenity, if he did not take away the natural element in his pieces by giving them a bombastic and confused style, and if he did not darken their beauty with an excess of art". This anonymous diatribe was the work of the journal's editor Johann Adolph Scheibe, who believed that music should above all be expressive and tasteful. Composers, he argued, should be aiming for simplicity in their music, writing melodies that were natural and unaffected. "Every single composer," Scheibe argued, "must sing in his thoughts."

Bach's clever and highly crafted music was simply out of tune with the times. The new age of the Enlightenment was dawning, and it favoured the simpler things in life: rational thought, clear explanation, beauty, order and balance. And it's these Enlightenment virtues that lie at the heart of music in the Classical era.

How did those philosophical differences change the sound of classical music? Whereas in the Baroque era an aria in an opera, or a movement from a concerto, stayed in one mood from beginning to end, mid-eighteenth century music positively encouraged changes of style, and a flexible approach to the way music developed. Sudden silences, abrupt changes of texture, and handbrake turns between moods of joy and turmoil were all new weapons in the Classical composer's armoury. Rather than being inherently serious, and often used in the service of religious worship, music now played the role of entertainment – the wider public wanted to listen to music for fun, and perform it for fun as well. This music was meant to be just as diverting to play as it was for audiences to enjoy. Phrases of music were structured much more simply – they had discernible beginnings and ends, just like sentences, and then they were woven into large-scale arguments which were the instrumental equivalent of conversations. One instrument might propose an idea which would then be debated and tossed around between others in the group. And of all the musical formats that were around in the Classical era, nothing exemplifies this conversational approach better than the string quartet – a lineup of two violins, viola and cello, all instruments derived from the same string family. Even if the first violin does grab a slightly bigger share of the musical limelight from the others, there is a sense of musical democracy in action, with all of the instruments able to have their say. Nobody has summed up the essence of this kind of music making better than Johann Wolfgang von Goethe (1749–1832), who memorably described a string quartet in action as "four rational people conversing."

Vienna led the way. The Austrian capital was brimming with gifted Italian musicians whose natural gift for melody was seized upon by Austrian and German composers. Austria itself was one of the most important European powers in the eighteenth century, and bristling with important people of power and influence, starting right at the very top with the Emperor Joseph II. Although he is remembered today for his "too many notes" remark to Mozart, Joseph II was in fact a keen and knowledgeable music lover, and a key figure of the Enlightenment. He banned the death penalty, fought against feudalism, promoted religious tolerance, and tried (and failed) to introduce universal compulsory education. Then there were the many leading aristocratic families who kept residences in Vienna; many of them had their own private orchestras and chamber music groups, and were passionate about music and generous in supporting it. Take Karl Alois, Prince Lichnowsky for example. He was a chamberlain at the Austrian court, and came from a major land-owning family with extensive estates in Silesia. Although he studied law, he was an amateur musician and composer, and a freemason – he was a member of the same lodge as Wolfgang Amadeus Mozart (1756–91). He lent Mozart money (which he never got back), and supported Ludwig van Beethoven (1770–1827) with a small annual allowance in the early 1800s.

That term "chamber music" refers to the fact that these small-scale works were designed to be performed in rooms at home. Chamber music also has an important technical meaning: it means that each part in the musical score is played by a single instrument, rather than a group of instruments as in, for example, the cello section of an orchestra. What this does is to place a burden of responsibility on the shoulders of each player. Not only is your individual contribution important, it is essential; other instruments rely on the notes that you play to fill in the harmony, and to give them their cue to play.

Going hand in hand with the conversational approach to works like these went a new way of developing form. The underlying sense of travel away from a home key – the tonic – and back again is something I discussed in the previous chapter. The Classical era adds something to this: it uses themes to advance the musical narrative. The musical ideas of this era don't just appear in a block; they are allowed to grow, develop, mutate, and give way to other ideas in much the same way as intellectual arguments might be tossed around between friends: many voices discussing one idea.

The past master of the Classical string quartet was Joseph Haydn (1732–1809) whose sixty-eight string quartets written over four decades are central to the genre. They combine tunefulness, logical development, surprises, and good humour in a superb musical cocktail.

Our chosen piece though is a string quartet by another of the Viennese greats: Mozart, who was a close friend of Haydn despite a twenty-four year age gap. Mozart wrote a set of six string quartets to pay tribute to his close friend: his so-called Haydn Quartets of the mid-1780s. They're very much in the style of the great man. It was after an informal play-through of one of these Mozart quartets in 1785 that Haydn said to Mozart's father Leopold: "Before God and as an honest man I tell you that your son is the greatest composer known to me either in person or by name; he has taste, and, furthermore, the most profound knowledge of composition." A tribute that Leopold proudly passed on in a letter to his daughter.

It's one of Mozart's Haydn Quartets that I'll take as the focus of this chapter: the B flat string quartet K458, nicknamed "The Hunt". A study of the first couple of minutes of this piece tells us a lot about how the great late eighteenth-century Viennese composers went about their business. The opening movement of quartets like these followed a formal procedure known as sonata form which falls into three sections. Musical ideas are introduced in the exposition; they are worked out and discussed in the development section; and summed up in the final section, the recapitulation. This thematic development, which takes place on top as it were, happens in conjunction with a harmonic journey underneath; the harmony moves from the tonic home key to several other key areas and back again. This is similar to what I discussed in the Baroque chapter, but by now it's reached a more sophisticated level. And to explain in more detail how this works, I'm going to examine just the first section of "The Hunt" quartet, up to the end of the exposition. To get the most out of this, I would encourage you to refer closely to a recording of the work. The timings below come from the Hagen Quartet's excellent recording on the Deutsche Grammophon label. Here's a blow by blow account of the opening section, with timing points:

00'00" – 00'12": the players launch straight into the first movement's main theme, which has a distinctive rhythm. An eighteenth-century pair of ears would recognise it as galloping along as horses do during a hunt, hence the quartet's nickname. The theme is stated clearly, two musical versions of the same phrase which are elegantly shaped and easy to identify – fitting in with the new credo of the Classical era, which liked music to follow the natural phrasing of speech. The two versions of the phrase are subtly different – one starts in the tonic, and ends up in the closest key area, the dominant; the second is a slightly ornamented version of the first – with a few added twiddles – and leads back to the tonic.

00'12" – 00'22": the lower three instruments continue the musical commentary, with the first violin answering. Again, this pattern happens twice, as in the opening section.

00'22" – 00'35": it is here that Mozart breaks out of the regular musical pattern he's established. The first violin takes the tail end of the phrase it's just played, and repeats it twice before the music hovers around in the dominant key area, briefly entering dreamland. This is a kind of breathing space you just don't find in music of the Baroque era, where there was always a strong sense of harmonic rhythm. Here, and in the Classical era in general, it's fine for music to be carried forward by themes rather than just harmony, and the sense of momentum is allowed to ebb and flow.

00'35" – 00'55": the main theme returns, this time led off by the lower instruments; the first violin is allowed to play a more independent and ornamental role on top.

00'55" – 01'12": there's a simple twiddle in the first violin part which is passed around down through all four instruments, right down to the cello and back up again. It's a perfect example of the Classical "conversational" approach in action, where each instrument is able to have its say. The twiddle is worked through a little further before the music comes to rest, not on the tonic, but on its nearest relative, the dominant – the key of F major in this case. All of this time, as well as the themes being developed, the harmony has been travelling too.

01'12" – 01'44": now that we are in the second key area, it's time for the second subject to be introduced. And the instrument chosen to do that is not the first violin which has had the lion's share of the spotlight, but the second violin. The theme that it introduces is also based on that twiddle – in a brilliant move by Mozart, it make its first appearance as the tail end of an idea, takes on a life of its own, and ends up becoming a theme in its own right – thematic development by the back door.

01'44" – 02'03": by this point we've been introduced to both main themes and have got to know them quite well. The harmonic journey has taken us from tonic to dominant, we feel quite secure in the new key, all of the ideas have been introduced, so this exposition section of the music could quite plausibly end there. But it doesn't; Mozart lingers a little longer, with an extended closing section called a coda. Then the music comes to rest with three chords in the dominant. The audience might have been expecting three loud closing chords in traditional fashion. But instead Mozart's closing chords surprisingly fade away to nothing – he marks them to be played pianissimo, or very quietly. This is a good example of Mozart challenging the conventions of the time, albeit in a subtle and understated way.

So that's the opening section of this movement. From that point, the exposition music is repeated, allowing us to familiarise ourselves with the musical argument a little more, before the players give it the full treatment in the development and recapitulation sections, with those main themes acting like protagonists in a drama. Why not listen through to the track in its entirety as if reading a novel, to find out what happens in the end?

CLASSICAL ERA – ESSENTIAL ELEMENTS:

balance and beauty
clear and elegant discussion of musical ideas
themes being developed in a structural way
avoiding extremes
plenty of conventions, often subtly contravened

FIVE TERMS TO KNOW:

Chamber music: small-scale works in which every part is played by just one instrument

Sonata form: a typical form of the Classical era for opening movements and sometimes closing ones as well, it arranges a piece into three sections of a musical argument: exposition, development and recapitulation

First subject, second subject: the principal themes or thematic groups in a sonata form movement it makes its first

Pianissimo: very quiet

Coda, codetta: passages that round off a section or a piece of music

The Romantic era
(1805–1910)

The year was 1812, with the Napoleonic wars heading towards their *dénouement*; the location, the fashionable spa town of Teplitz in Bohemia. Taking a stroll together were two of the greatest creative figures of the age: one, the eminent poet and playwright Johann von Goethe; the other, the composer Ludwig van Beethoven, who was in town to take the waters on doctor's orders. The two men saw none other than the Austrian Empress and her retinue walking towards them. Goethe did the normal thing in such circumstances – he took his hat off and moved to one side to let them pass. Beethoven though said: "Keep walking as you are; they must make way for us, not the other way around".

That little anecdote may or may not be true – it's been passed down by Bettina von Arnim, a mutual friend of Beethoven and Goethe with a colourful imagination. But it's an incident that could very well have taken place. At a time when musicians and artists were little more than servants, and forelocks had to be dutifully tugged, Beethoven was ruthlessly egalitarian. Another story which has more chance of being true: when Beethoven arrived in Vienna in his early twenties to make his name, his first patron was Prince Lichnowsky who cropped up in the previous chapter. He set the young composer up with an apartment, social connections, and even an annual income. Later in life, when the Prince used to climb the four flights of stairs to Beethoven's apartment and listen to him play, he had to do so sitting outside on the landing, because Beethoven would never let him in. A classic example of biting the hand that feeds him. But Beethoven's argument was: why should he show deference to noblemen? He was every bit their equal.

At a time when all of Europe was in turmoil, Beethoven was completely in tune with the revolutionary spirit of the age. He was a great supporter of Napoleon, the personification of the new Republican ideals of liberty, equality and fraternity. Beethoven even went so far as to compose a symphony in Napoleon's honour. But when Napoleon proclaimed himself Emperor of the French in May 1804, Beethoven felt personally betrayed, and angrily changed the name of his new symphony to turn it into a more general depiction of heroism: the Eroica Symphony. It's an innovative work in many ways: its direct engagement with the politics of the time; its length – the first movement on its own is as long as most symphonies of the time; and its musical fabric, which is woven from several melodic fragments rather than a couple of main themes. And that's why I have taken the year Beethoven's Eroica Symphony was premiered – 1805 – as my starting point for the Romantic era. Having learned the ropes from other composers in Vienna, Beethoven developed a brilliantly arresting style of his own – original, dramatic, and heroic – before later turning inwards and writing music that was beautiful, sublime and mysterious, partly influenced by the deafness which profoundly affected his last decades.

Beethoven died in 1827, leaving the next generation of composers with a tough act to follow – in two respects. Firstly there's the music. He had expanded and developed all of the Classical-era genres – symphony, opera, string quartet, sonata – treating them with brilliance and individuality. How could you improve on Beethoven's example? Secondly there's his approach to music in general. Beethoven was investing his symphonies, sonatas and string quartets with everything in life that mattered most to him.

This was a man who wasn't writing to order, or playing to entertain his social superiors. This is a man who used music to express his own personal struggles, or a wider concern with humanity and freedom. He lived through his music – and that's what made him more than a great composer. In the true Romantic sense of the term, Beethoven was an artist.

So where next? Some nineteenth-century composers opted to continue with the forms and style that Haydn and Mozart had brought to perfection in the Classical era. Although they occasionally enriched their work with outside influences from literature or art, composers such as Schumann, Mendelssohn and Brahms kept the logic of the music itself as the essence of their work. These composers were champions of absolute music – music which made sense on its own terms, without aiming to represent anything else, such as a picture or a storyline – and as such had men such as the tremendously influential Edouard Hanslick batting for their side. In his important 1854 book "On the Beautiful in Music," Hanslick argued that composers should continue to work in the tradition of Mozart and Beethoven, and that the value of music lay in music alone – "Music alone consists of successions and forms of sound, and these alone constitute the subject; it must develop gradually with intelligible and organic definiteness, as buds develop into rich blossoms." Hanslick and co found themselves in a passionate debate which became known as the "War of the Romantics" – for them, the enemy camp were those who believed in the Music of the Future. This second group took Beethoven's innovations and ran with them, blazing a striking trail of musical innovation through the nineteenth century. The composer had stopped being a craftsman and started being an artist, and often the music became about them. Look no further than Hector Berlioz (1803–69) for a striking early example of this. The semi-autobiographical Symphonie fantastique of 1830 took Berlioz's own spurned love for an ideal woman as its starting point. Its hero tries to commit suicide by overdosing on opium, only to have horrible visions of being led to the scaffold and seeing his beloved swept up in a witches' orgy. Which is just about as far from courtly Vienna as you could get! Later came Franz Liszt (1811–86), virtuoso pianist and sex symbol, and brilliantly forward-looking composer who told stories through his orchestral music in the form of symphonic poems; and Richard Wagner (1813–83), famously expansive operatic composer and a veritable one man band of theatrical creativity, who brought together all of the arts and sought to make a perfect blend of them all: a Gesamtkunstwerk.

And then there is Gustav Mahler (1860–1911). A child of the Austrian Empire, he was born into a poor German-speaking Jewish family in Bohemia and rose through the musical ranks thanks to plenty of hard work and determination. At the time of his death in Vienna, he had recently finished a ten-year tenure as director of the prestigious Court Opera, and taken up appointments in the United States as director of the Metropolitan Opera and the New York Philharmonic. A rags to riches journey, in musical terms. Mahler's achievement was immense; he was both a thoroughly hands-on practical musician and one of the Romantic era's most significant composers and saw no dividing line between music and life in his own work. For him, the symphony must be like the world – embracing everything, all of man's concerns – love and death and his fears and aspirations. Sometimes the music in his nine completed symphonies is banal, sometimes it's intense, sometimes at peace, at other times unbalanced and hysterical. But, as Mahler might have put it – "that's life." And the core issues in Mahler's music are just as relevant to a twenty-first century postmodern audience as they were in the turmoil of Mahler's own fin de siècle Vienna, where the belief in conventional religion and traditional social values was very much on the wane. Ferdinand Pfohl, who knew Mahler well, described him as "a mystic, a God-seeker. His imagination circled endlessly around God and the world, around life and death, around spiritual matters and nature. Eternity and eternal life were at the centre of his thoughts. He wanted to believe – belief at any price."

It's interesting that while other forward-looking composers created new forms for their new musical approaches – "new wine needs new bottles," as Liszt put it – Mahler kept faith with the traditional formal framework of the symphony and invested it with his brilliant and wide-ranging ideas – both that great search for spirituality, but also less lofty aspects of "the world": sounds which are on the face of it, brash, coarse or mundane – what you might call the base metal of musical materials. Popular music is everywhere in Mahler; whether it's brash fanfares or poignant nursery rhymes, they are an essential part of the fabric of each of his symphonies. Often they draw on painful memories from Mahler's unhappy childhood. Once, after a beating from his father, Mahler ran into the street, where he came across a military band being put through its paces – forging a lifelong link in his mind between high drama and the mundanity of public music from that point onwards. The importance of nature in his music stems from another incident with his father. Once when the two of them were out walking, his father remembered he had to finish some task at home. He left the young Gustav sitting on a log, promising to return to him – but then he forgot. Four hours later, he returned, finding Mahler absolutely transfixed by the sounds and the sheer beauty of Nature. And those two sound worlds appear side by side within the first two minutes of the work I'm choosing as my musical focus of the Romantic era: Mahler's Symphony no 1, composed in the late 1880s. Its opening bars take place in some mysterious outdoor space – a forest clearing perhaps? The opening bars are marked "wie ein Naturlaut" – like a sound of nature – with the call of a cuckoo competing with distant military fanfares. It's a magical evocation – for me it sums up a paradox in Mahler's music; it seeks to engage with the world and escape from it at the same time. For the American composer Aaron Copland, writing in "Our New Music" of 1941, Mahler was "by nature a profoundly childlike artist, yet heir to all the problematic complexities of the modern world."

The main theme of the first movement arrives at 03'14" in my chosen recording. The cello section introduces a theme taken from the opening song of Mahler's *Lieder eines Fahrenden Gesellen*. The song describes one of those lovely spring mornings when all seems right in the world; a finch tweets (in the old-fashioned sense) to a young man walking through the fields, while bluebells ring out their own greeting to him – but he can't be happy because he's lovesick. If you fast forward to the end of the song cycle, you'll find him lying down under a tree. Resting, or dying? The text is ambiguous. The symphony is imbued with the mood of these songs, and that's another example of Mahler's total view of music – his songs are integrated into his symphonies, as is the meaning behind them, often dealing, as I've said, with the things he cared most about in life: love and death, innocence and spirituality.

Death is especially important in Mahler – eight of his fourteen siblings died before reaching adulthood – and the third movement of his First Symphony opens with a striking take on childhood innocence. Mahler quotes the nursery tune Bruder Martin – the one we know as Frère Jacques – but with a double dose of darkness. It's played high up on the double bass, creating a sound that is supposed to be uncomfortable and eerie; and he recasts the melody in a minor key. This is a nursery rhyme overladen with

The Huntsman's Funeral Procession. A woodcut by Moritz von Schwind which inspired the third movement of Mahler's First Symphony.

tragedy. Listen to the music unfolding over the first couple of minutes of the third movement and you'll hear what I mean.

I've pointed out a few of the clear references in the music – but what is the First Symphony as a whole trying to say? Mahler circulated a programme for his symphony in 1900 before its Vienna premiere, painting a prose picture of a man who is both heroic and vulnerable, locked in battle with the forces of Fate. Themes representing nature, innocence and death I've already pointed out. And the drama of the symphony comes to a head in the last movement, the finale. In a movement once entitled "From the Inferno to Paradise" Mahler describes the hero conquering his demons and returning to the happiness of his youth, in a symphonic trajectory which starts in the first minute with a representation of orchestral turmoil, and works its way towards the most triumphant resolution.

After the premiere of the symphony in Budapest on the 21st November 1889, the critic August Beer claimed that it was only Mahler's friends who had been applauding the "incomprehensible and disagreeable cacophony" they'd just heard. For him it had merely been a "succession of formless, impersonal, atmospheric tableaux." Acceptance was slow in coming; Mahler's music never

29

gained a foothold in concert programmes during his lifetime, and the Nazis did their best to suppress it in succeeding decades. But ever since the 1960s his works have been an essential part of any symphonic season. A combination of genre-defying musical imagination; some stunning scoring from a man who knew the possibilities of the symphony orchestra inside out; and the way Mahler puts his own personal concerns about the greatest questions of life right at the heart of his music; it's for those reasons that I've chosen Gustav Mahler as my quintessential composer of the nineteenth century. And his First Symphony is a great starting point for anyone's Romantic exploration.

ROMANTIC ERA – ESSENTIAL ELEMENTS:

Composers had become artists – and some even became heroes of their own work

Some composers worked within the Classical forms and styles, enriching them with a new expressive dimension; others set out on a relentless search for the new, expanding genres to the limit and creating new genres to accommodate their new ideas

Music became less self-contained; it borrowed from literature, painting, politics, and even the colourful lives of its own composers

FIVE TERMS TO KNOW:

Programme music: music that's designed to tell a story or paint a picture.

Absolute music – music that isn't! It's there to succeed on its own terms: themes, an organic musical narrative, and structure – it's all self-contained.

Gesamtkunstwerk: Wagner's idea of bringing several disciplines together to make a perfect, all-embracing art form.

Symphony: a musical genre for orchestra, usually made up of four movements or sections. The movements may be separated but they're designed to hang together and take us on a journey – purely musical or sometimes with an element or programme music – see above.

Symphonic poem or tone poem: a piece of narrative programme music painted on an orchestral canvas, borrowing elements from the form of a symphony, but in order to tell a story or sketch out elements of it.

Terrific Uproar: a violent interlude
(1913)

The date is the 29th of May 1913; the venue, the brand-new Théâtre des Champs-Élysées in Paris; the occasion, the most scandalous ballet premiere of the twentieth century; and the performers, the Ballets Russes, brainchild of the Russian impresario Sergei Diaghilev. With a succession of brilliant new works and innovative stagings, Diaghilev and the Ballet Russes were giving the elegant and institutionalised French ballet world a sharp kick in the *derrière*.

Le Sacre du printemps, the Rite of Spring – or Весна священная if you prefer – is the story of a Russian virgin being sacrificed to appease the god of spring. So perhaps this was never going to be an easy-going spectacle. Diaghilev's inspired production team included the genius dancer Vaslav Nijinsky and the young composer Igor Stravinsky (1882–1971) – the scenario had appeared to Stravinsky in a dream – and in their hands Le Sacre became something stunning and shocking. In creating his choreography, Nijinsky gave his dancers deliberately ugly movements while Stravinsky came up with countless musical innovations that puzzled the audience right from the outset.

What is the instrument we hear playing solo in the bleak opening bars? The critic of the literary periodical *Gil Blas*, Georges Pioch, thought it must an oboe; his neighbour thought it was a muted trumpet – and he was a distinguished conductor, so he ought to know. They were both wrong; Le Sacre's striking opening is played by a solo bassoon, the deepest member of the woodwind section – almost unrecognisable because Stravinsky asks it to play unusually high, and right out of its register, or tessitura, to use the musical term. It's the first of dozens of examples of Stravinsky rethinking the possibilities of classical music – avoiding the well-trodden Austro-German path which I've outlined in the previous chapter, and turning to a new source in the desire to create a new sound world: Russian folk music, and the raw and primitive elements of its folk culture.

Sounds like that were never going to sit well with a large part of the clientele of the Théâtre des Champs-Élysées that night. The bejewelled ballet and music establishment were there in force, seated in boxes, elegant in white gloves, and resplendent in diamonds and pearls. Also in the audience were some passionate supporters of the Ballets Russes, many of whom were artists themselves – painters, poets, journalists and musicians. Valentine Gross was one of them – she knew that the new ballet was going to be unconventional, but said: "I was expecting neither such a great work of art, or such a scandal. The theatre seemed to be shaken by an earthquake." People hissed, howled, and shouted insults. It was one of the most scandalous evenings in the history of ballet, and of classical music – the press dubbed it Le Massacre du printemps. What did Diaghilev make of how the ballet had been received? His only recorded remark is that it was "exactly what I wanted."

The impulse behind the creation of Le Sacre du printemps has lain behind so much of the way that contemporary classical music has developed in the intervening decades. I'm talking about its desire to innovate, to intrigue, to shock, all accompanied by the sound of rulebooks being unceremoniously torn up. This time round, there was no one way forward for classical music – it exploded in a

PARISIANS HISS
NEW BALLET

Russian Dancer's Latest Offering, "The Consecration of Spring," a Failure.

HAS TO TURN UP LIGHTS

Manager of Theatre Takes This Means to Stop Hostile Demonstrations as Dance Goes On.

Report on the première of Le Sacre du printemps in the *New York Times*, June 8th, 1913

number of different directions – but if there was a root cause behind all of this innovation, it was the need to break away from what had gone before. Romanticism had run its course. The system of harmonic travelling and homecoming had been pushed to its limits by Wagner, Mahler and others, and that formal principle did indeed break down because of the way music was developing, or over-extending itself. Add to that the heady mix of emotion and sometimes self-obsession in its greatest composers, and the whole thing simply sounded overblown in the cold light of the early twentieth century.

For the most part in this crash course on classical music I've been talking so far only about the Austrian and German school of composing – for the very good reason that for so long this is the most important stream of classical composition. But towards the end of the nineteenth century things slowly began to change, with the rise in nationalism. As smaller countries fought for the right to govern themselves all over Europe, interest grew in the folk music from these countries. So we have Hungarian Dances being composed by Brahms for example, Czech music made popular with composers such as Dvořák (1841–1904) and Janáček (1854–1928) – and raw sounds from the Russian folk tradition.

For me, Russia is the most interesting example of all. It was slightly cut off from the rest of Europe, and initially backward by comparison; at the start of the Romantic era, beyond the exclusive

34

confines of the Imperial Opera Houses, orchestral music was almost entirely run and written by a few brilliant aristocratic amateurs. In fact, if it hadn't been for their passionate enthusiasm, Russia's own distinctive style of music would never have got off the ground. They were self-taught, since Russia had no conservatoires to speak of. But that lack of training also proved to be a boon, forcing composers to develop their own idiosyncratic musical styles, and, as a result, Russia produced some of the most distinctive and individual music of the time. And when conservatoires did finally arrive in the 1860s, establishing a tradition of excellence in performance and composition which continues to this day, Russia was in a great position to catch up. Five of its leading composers formed a breakaway group of leading Russian composers known as the Mighty Handful – or simply the Five. They strongly believed that their country's music education system shouldn't just be churning out pale imitations of German composers; the time had come for Russia to develop music in a way that was characteristically Russian. As their guiding light the critic Vladimir Stasov memorably put it, "it was time for the hoop skirts and tailcoats of the Petersburg élites to make way for the long Russian coats of the provinces." The whole thing went hand in hand with a renewed interest in peasant art and culture in the 1870s, with the composers developing their own kind of Romantic music using folk melodies, exotic storylines, and shimmering orchestration.

So when the big musical change came, and the excesses of Romanticism went out of the window, Russian music was well placed to adapt in the new modernist era. Because shocking though Stravinsky's Le Sacre was, it was rooted in the kind of sound world that the Russian generation of composers before Stravinsky had spent the last few decades developing. Nikolai Rimsky-Korsakov (1844–1908) was one of them, a composer with a great melodic gift, and a self-taught skill for writing brilliantly for orchestra. Stravinsky studied with Rimsky-Korsakov for three years with the specific aim of mastering the technical aspects of writing music, and distilled what he learnt into his own compositional style. Orchestral colour "is the very essence of the composition, not its mere dressing-up," according to Rimsky-Korsakov, and that comment could be applied to any of the three great ballet scores that Stravinsky went on to write for Diaghilev's Ballets Russes from 1910 onwards: L'Oiseau de feu, about a magnificent Firebird with magical powers; Petrushka, about a puppet taking on a life of its own at a glitteringly icy Russian fair; and this one, Le Sacre. The reason I've chosen to concentrate on it is because in so many respects the score the audience heard on that dramatic night in May 1913 was to shape the future of music in the decades to come. Let's have a look at it in more detail now, from the point of view of its four main musical ingredients: melody, rhythm, harmony and orchestration.

Le Sacre grew out of a vision Stravinsky had in 1910 of "a solemn pagan rite: sage elders, seated in a circle, watching a young girl dance herself to death. They were sacrificing her to appease the god of spring." That remarkable bassoon opening we've already covered. Other wind instruments then join in — first a horn, then deep clarinets and a mellow-toned cor anglais. But for the most part their lines run alongside each other, without fitting in harmonically. This is horizontal music; the chords that the lines make don't really matter. The sense I get from this opening is of animal calls in nature, being uttered but not interacting. Or possibly what we have here is a kind of musical version of the Russian language. It's a technique that a few composers from Eastern Europe had used — Mussorgsky (1839–81) for example, and Janáček: creating wordless folksongs that imitate the rhythms of Russian speech.

After the horizontal melodic strands of that two-minute opening comes a completely different musical texture. Stravinsky called the second movement of Le Sacre The Augurs of Spring, and it begins with what can best be described as a musical pile-up. In the middle ground of the texture is a dominant seventh chord of E flat. Below it, in the bass, a three-note chord of F flat. Two chords just a semitone apart in pitch: when they are played together, the effect is brutal. Stravinsky reuses this sound relentlessly throughout the movement; firstly in a succession of choppy chords which occasionally leap out at you in unguessable rhythms. And then in spread-out arpeggios played by low bassoons and cor anglais – this first appears around ten seconds in. The repeated figure played by the wind instruments here is something that's know as an ostinato – the Italian word for obstinate, which describes the obsessive way a pattern of notes comes back. Stravinsky gives us no indication of when the music will jump from one section to the other – as listeners we are kept on our toes, perhaps every bit as much as the dancers are. This is development by contrast and surprise, completely different from the organic approach of developing a theme which had become so familiar in the hands of previous generations of composers. With the rough and alarming sound of the music in our minds, again just think back to that Parisian premiere, where Le Sacre was first performed hot on the heels of Les Sylphides, set to music by Chopin that was as genteel as you could get!

Harmony and orchestration are next, and let's look at them both together, taking the extraordinary opening of Part Two of Le Sacre as our focus. It's another mysterious introduction, this time to the ceremony of choosing the girl who is about to dance herself to death. This movement is predominantly quiet – the loudest indication is only for the players to play "mf" or quite loudly – and yet Stravinsky involves almost every instrument in his huge orchestra in this section. Not only that, he divides the instruments of the string sections into further subdivisions, and asks them to use mutes on their instruments, floating bow strokes, and occasionally to play harmonics, an effect which produces a light and glassy sound from the strings. So the overall sense is of vast power being held in reserve; the textures are amazingly subtle, and their effect is even stronger after the savagery of some of the music beforehand. Stravinsky is a master of combining the forces of the orchestra like this – the art of orchestration, the musical equivalent of how an artist combines and mixes colours on a palette. In terms of the harmony, Stravinsky immediately confronts us with a delicious problem. The first thing we hear from the horns at the very start is a long sustained chord of D minor. Above it, in the wind section, there's an undulating figure which is based exactly a semitone away in D sharp minor. That's as close as possible in pitch, but the notes of the two chords played together – as in the Augurs of Spring earlier – don't make sense when heard together. Not in the traditional tonal sense anyway. There's a hint of bitonality here – music being in two different keys at once. But when the instrumental colours are chosen with such care, and the chords are voiced as expertly as this, it's music which works not as two clashing chords, but as one composite creation, full of richness and mystery.

And the last excerpt I'll leave you with is the finale. It takes us back to brutality, as the unfortunate virgin meets her violent end. Rhythm comes to the forefront again here, but this time there is no ostinato to keep us on the straight and narrow. The rhythms are ever-changing and deliberately debilitating. Its time signatures – the numbers indicating whether beats in the bar are short or long, and how many there are – are deliberately all over the place. Interestingly, when playing this piece as a teenaged violinist, I found the rhythms difficult to learn at first, but once I had absorbed them they stayed learnt, and I've lived with them ever since. The irregularity of Stravinsky's music in Le Sacre du printemps is one of the things that makes it unforgettable.

TERRIFIC UPROAR: A VIOLENT INTERLUDE —
FIVE TERMS TO KNOW:

Timbre: the quality of a note produced by a musical instrument.

Tessitura: the range of an instrument.

Bitonal: having more than one tonal centre.

Ostinato: a repeated rhythmic figure.

Diatonic: based round a tonal centre.

The Last Hundred Years
(1915–2015)

The dramatic premiere of Le Sacre du printemps has gone down in history as one of the most momentous evenings in the history of classical music. Not only did its scandalous success greatly enhance the fame of Stravinsky, Diaghilev and the Ballets Russes, it also played its part in changing the course of music. The link with the immediate Romantic past had been broken, freeing composers up to seek out new ways of writing music that would reflect the spirit of those rapidly-changing times. But Le Sacre also presented them with a problem: in some respects it was hard to surpass what Stravinsky had created. That blood-curdling finale in particular, with its random rhythms and shrieking sounds: how was it possible to write anything more violent and extreme than that?

Classical music did though find a way of moving forward. Several ways, in fact, and in this final chapter I'll be sketching out the most important routes that composers have taken over the last hundred years. Whereas the musical approaches in the eras I've outlined in previous chapters have been fairly unified and consistent, the last century has seen an explosion of ideas and philosophies, with composers striking out in a number of different directions. In the first part of this chapter I will be summarising some of the most important ways of composing, before homing in on one work written in the late 1980s which exemplifies some of the most important recent trends: for me, a contemporary masterpiece.

It makes sense, though, to restart with Stravinsky, with the powerful last punch of Le Sacre du printemps still reverberating in our ears. For him, its extreme violence was as far as he ever went in that direction. The next step for him was in fact to take a step back: not to the nineteenth century, but to the two musical epochs before that, the music of the Baroque and Classical eras, where, as we've learnt, emotions were kept in check and there was an objective interest in form and clarity. Pulcinella (1920) is a great example of this. Stravinsky hand-picked some themes by the Italian Baroque composer Giovanni Pergolesi (1710–36) as the source material and starting point for another ballet for Serge Diaghilev, this time based on a pantomime-like *commedia dell'arte* story. For Stravinsky, it was an enormously important commission. "Pulcinella was my discovery of the past," he said, "the epiphany through which the whole of my late work became possible."

What Stravinsky is describing there is one of the early twentieth century's first important composing trends – a style known as neoclassicism, blending the detached clarity of music from the eighteenth century with a contemporary je ne sais quoi. Other leading exponents include the witty and brilliant Frenchman Francis Poulenc (1899–1963) - and also the Hungarian composer Béla Bartók (1881–1945). More important than the lean textures and detached sound of neoclassicism for Bartók though was the possibilities that folk music offered. Composers had used Eastern European folk tunes before, but generally in a cosmetic way, as local colour in their compositions; Bartók took this music much more seriously, working hard as what we might call an ethnomusicologist these days; for him it was a fertile source of catchy rhythms, unusual scales and fascinating "wrong-note" harmonies.

Another approach was to break free from the time-worn system of tonal harmony, and develop completely new ways of organising notes. After all, in the closing decades of the nineteenth century composers had been writing music with such lush harmonies and sophisticated chords that the tonal system had been creaking at the seams anyway – check out Richard Wagner's Tristan and Isolde Prelude for a great example of that. It was Arnold Schoenberg (1874–1951) who arrived at a system of composing that did away with the idea of a tonal centre altogether. In his hands, every pitch was now of equal importance, a sort of musical Marxism. This concept goes by the name of serialism, dodecaphony, or simply twelve-tone music, so-called because within each musical scale there are twelve possible notes to choose from. By organising them in a horizontal row or series, a melody could be created which could be played straight, flipped upside down or turned backwards, while superimposing them vertically could provide harmony. Either way the idea was that no one note could be "more important" than any of the others. Schoenberg was freeing them from the constraint of having to fit into a chord; he called it his "emancipation of the dissonance."

Other important composers who pushed the boundaries in this way include the American composer John Cage (1912–92). He started composing in a serial style, before breaking free of the strict control of this method in the 1950s to create work that stretched the very definition of music itself. His works for prepared piano for example, a normal instrument which had been altered in various ways, from nails being stuck into the hammers to bits of wood jammed between the strings, to create a range of colourful sounds; and his music inspired by Indian philosophy, Zen Buddhism and the I Ching which introduced an element of chance. Most famously he composed 4'33" for any instrument; the staves on the score are completely blank, and Cage instructs the performer not to play at all for the entire duration of the piece.

Then there were new ways of creating musical pitches using electronic sounds – most intriguingly in the hands of Karlheinz Stockhausen (1928–2007). A breakthrough work of his was Gesang der Jünglinge, or, literally, "Song of the Youths" of 1955–56. It's been described as "the first masterpiece of electronic music," and it's important because it seamlessly matches electronic sounds - sine tones and clicks - with the recorded voice of a twelve year old boy, in a setting of an ecstatic moment from the Biblical Book of Daniel; it describes how Nebuchadnezzar throws Shadrach, Meshach, and Abednego into a burning fiery furnace from which they miraculously emerge unharmed. The outlandish scope of that piece is entirely in keeping with the composer. Stockhausen once had a dream that four string players were playing a quartet, each of them flying above the ground in separate helicopters. He woke up and made that dream reality, and I've heard the end result played live, as the centrepiece of his opera Mittwoch aus Licht, which was given its world premiere in 2012 as part of the Cultural Olympiad.

Still, the tradition of writing recognisable melodies in a home key, or tunes you can hum, didn't die out altogether in the twentieth century. Far from it; the American composer Aaron Copland (1900–1990) had a road to Damascus moment during the Great Depression in the 1930s. Realising that his countrymen needed music that they could relate with to help them through those difficult times, he turned his back on the complex intellectual music he'd been writing up to that time and sought to say what he had to say, as he put it, "in the simplest possible terms," in works which were both accessible and contemporary; pieces like Fanfare for the Common Man of 1942, later made popular by the rock band Emerson, Lake and Palmer, and the ballet score Appalachian Spring of 1944. While in Britain, we had Britten – Benjamin Britten (1913–1976), who wrote right across the board from anyone from children and amateurs through to the most highly-skilled professionals. In his masterful operas in particular, he showed how he could write modern music that fully embraced singable melodies, set to plots centred around the loss of innocence and the struggle of the individual against a hostile world. And over in the former Soviet Union, Dmitri Shostakovitch (1906–1975) wrote music in an expressive and heroic mould which has been criticised in some quarters for being Romantic and old-fashioned – and yet it expresses the atmosphere of living in a totalitarian state in a creative artistic way which no other composer has equalled.

Then there's the style of composition known as minimalism, which first emerged in New York in the early 1960s, with structures based on repeating patterns of notes which gradually change over time. What sets minimalism apart from the other new trends I've outlined is that it quickly established itself as a form of new music which was immediately comprehensible and appealing, thanks to its sound world which is much more akin to pop music. Leading lights of this movement include Terry Riley (b. 1935), John Adams (b. 1947), and Philip Glass (b. 1937) whose work also spills over into writing music for movies – he's written over fifty film scores. American minimalism has found its counterpart in the Baltic states in the work of composers such as Arvo Pärt (b. 1935), who composes in a radically simplified style. His music reduces music back to its bare essentials, often right down to the simple triad, or three-note chord. You can't get much more minimal than that – a kind of compositional simplicity in which even the subtle reverberation of a single chord takes on a deep spiritual meaning.

Minimalism doesn't have to mean simple, though: it can embrace layers of complex musical structures at the same time, and it can be used to express thoughts that delve well below the superficial, even taking on some of the most profound issues of the human experience. And that's the case with the work in focus in this final chapter, by Steve Reich (b. 1936). Not only is he one of the greatest of all American composers, he's also the only composer featured in this volume who regularly wears a baseball cap. In 1988 Reich wrote a fascinating piece called Different Trains. Blending elements of recorded speech and music for string quartet, it's a work which tells a deeply personal story, drawing parallels between his own upbringing and that of Jewish children growing up in Europe at the same time, who were seized by the German Army during the Second World War. I'll be examining the background and the technique of this piece, and also stepping back to reflect on Reich's role in developing the style of music which we know as minimalism.

Steve Reich was born in New York in 1936, the son of a Jewish father, Leonard, and a mother named June Sillman, who was a Broadway lyricist and singer. His parents got divorced when Steve was just one year old, and his father moved to Los Angeles. So as the young Steve grew up, he became quite accustomed to shuttling between the two cities on long coast-to-coast train journeys. As far as music went, he took piano lessons as a child, but says it was very much a case of the "middle-class favorites" – he hardly came across any music outside the late eighteenth and nineteenth centuries. Then in his early teens, several new music discoveries hit him like a thunderbolt – he heard the Fifth Brandenburg Concerto by Bach, Stravinsky's Le Sacre du printemps, and the new jazz sound of bebop, and it changed the course his life.

The next fifteen years or so saw Steve Reich learning how to play drums so that he could play jazz; taking up a place at Cornell University to study philosophy; studying composition at Juilliard in New York while hanging out at jazz clubs at night trying to hear John Coltrane as much as he could; and working towards a master's degree in composition in San Francisco. This was the early 1960s, when the twelve-tone system of composing that I mentioned earlier was very much in vogue; it's a system that Reich used at the very start of his composing career, but never really got along with. The new and characteristically American musical style of minimalism was just coming into being in downtown New York at that time, Manhattan's Lower East Side to be exact, which was a world apart from the complexities of serial music. In minimalist music, simplicity was a virtue – Terry Riley's In C of 1964 is a piece that Reich was involved with as a performer from the very outset, and it's a great early example; it starts with a simple C major chord, and other notes emerge out of it in repeated melodic phrases. A work like that pared music down to its essentials and wasn't on the face of it hard to understand – so a new strong bond emerged between composers, performers and their audience.

Minimalism was helped on its way by plenty of trial and error – and fortuitous technical accidents. One day Reich found himself playing the same recording on two different tape machines; as it turned out, they were running at slightly different speeds, which meant the recordings went in and out of phase with each other. The effect was so powerful that he went on to use it in It's Gonna Rain (1965) and Come Out (1966) – two major works which are well worth a listen.

There's one more element to add into the creative mix; around this time Reich came across a book of transcriptions of drumming from Ghana. What leapt off the page for Reich was the fact that so much of the music was based on patterns of 12, and the way its subdivisions of three, four, and six interacted with each other. To explore this further, Reich organised a five week research trip to

Ghana where he studied with the master drummer Gideon Alorwoyie, and distilled some of what he learnt into Drumming (1971), a piece scored for tuned and untuned percussion instruments which lasts for about an hour. What's fascinating about Drumming is that although the basic rhythmic layout stays the same throughout, Reich gradually transforms the musical colour of the piece very gradually over time.

So, the essence of minimalism in patterns; harmonic simplicity, complex rhythms – and the meditative power of repetition in music that changes only very slowly and almost imperceptibly: that's the essence of Steve Reich's early development – and the backstory if you like to the piece in focus here: Different Trains.

In 1976 Reich married the video artist Beryl Korot, and began to explore his Jewish identity in a series of works over the next decade, an era in which his popularity grew and grew. He even sold out a concert of his own music at Carnegie Hall in 1980 – the first time this had ever been done. Not only was he forging a new creative path, he was taking a new and large audience with him on his journey. After Reich has been asked to write a piece for the Kronos Quartet, it was Beryl Korot who suggested that he should use a sampler in it. He'd recently been given five of these new instruments by the Casio Company, and was getting excited about the possibilities. Electronic music and synthesisers no longer had any appeal for Reich; he much preferred working with real voices and instruments. But samplers, devices which could record and play back actual sounds, were a different story – especially the way they could bring non-musical material into musical settings.

The piece of equipment that Reich was working with was a Casio FZ1 sampling keyboard; though it might have been impressive for its time, its capacity these days seems almost laughably limited. It

47

came with a one megabyte memory, a tiny fraction of what's available on a present day smartphone. At its highest quality setting it could only record samples of up to 15 seconds, no more. Still, back in the '80s, the FZ1 and machines like it opened up a whole new realm of possibilities. Pop musicians had been using samplers for years, but in the contemporary classical world, this was a first.

Given that this piece is now such an established contemporary music classic, it's interesting to chart the progress of this piece as it gradually came together. Reich knew he wanted to write a piece for sampled voices and strings, but his first idea was to create a work around the great Béla Bartók who'd spent the last five years of his life in America. Then he changed tack in favour of something based on the philosopher Ludwig Wittgenstein; after all, Reich has written a thesis on Wittgenstein back in his Cornell University days. But it turned out that no recordings of his voice were available.

It was at this point that Reich realised that the answer to his search lay closer to home. He thought back to those train trips that he'd taken as a child between New York and Los Angeles. They took place between 1939 and 1941, and he realised that at the same time over in Europe, young Jewish boys just like him were being put on trains headed for Poland - and they never came back.

Reich sought out two interviewees who could bear witness to the American rail trips; one was a lady he knew well called Virginia Mitchell who'd looked after him as a child, and another was a Pullman porter who had worked on exactly that rail route at the time, by the name of Lawrence Davis. Reich recorded them as they talked about their experiences at the time, chose just a few fragments of their phrases that had grabbed his attention, isolated

them, and used them as a framework for the piece. Different
Trains is a piece in three sections. If you listen to the start of the
first of them, you'll hear how Virginia Mitchell then Lawrence
Davis share their memories over a backdrop of percussive string
quartet chords and sounds sampled from the real world – train
sirens and bells.

What I think is fascinating about Reich's way of working in
Different Trains is that the spoken phrases aren't being pinned
onto the music – they're generating the notes that the instruments
play. The way the voices imply a kind of speech melody make it a
kind of modern day version of Sprechgesang, the vocal technique
somewhere in between speech and song that Arnold Schoenberg
had introduced just before the First World War. I love the way the
instruments set up each vocal entry by changing key and rhythm
and establishing a pattern, before we get to hear the source phrase
itself. Reich established a basic rule for himself: that every time a
woman speaks, the viola doubles her voice; every time a man
speaks, he's doubled by the cello; and the violins always overlay
the sound of the train whistles. The pitch and speed of the train
sounds may be altered to fit the music, a train sample might even
be reversed now and again, but Reich leaves the sound of the
words unaltered, so that it's language and human testimony that
control the piece, not musical technique.

We've covered the American side of the story; to find European
voices relating their experiences of the Holocaust, Reich went up
to Yale University to delve into its substantial Holocaust archive.
He spent two riveting days there listening through to survivors
talking about what they'd gone through, and again he went
through the material with great care, extracting telling phrases
which had musical qualities and which also convey something
concise and meaningful. He chose testimony from three survi-

vors; two women named Rachella and Rachel, and a man named Paul. In the second movement of Different Trains, entitled "During the War," we hear testimony from all three of them, describing how the Germans marched into Holland and Hungary – and invaded their lives.

One thing that Reich's music doesn't generally major on is textural variety – enormous contrast between light and shade. That's true of most of the music in Different Trains, but things do change towards the very end of the work, as Reich lightens the texture and brings in a real transparency to the quartet sound. At this point in the Different Trains narrative, the Second World War is a thing of the past, but in the work's closing minutes, the voice of a Holocaust survivor returns, with a reflection of how the power of music can endure in the most terrible of circumstances. Rachella recalls how in the concentration camp where she was being held, "There was one girl, who had a beautiful voice … and they loved to listen to the singing, the Germans … and when she stopped singing they said, 'More, more' and they applauded."

THE LAST HUNDRED YEARS – ESSENTIAL ELEMENTS:

Music being pushed to the brink and a whole variety of approaches emerging, some radical and others conservative: neo-classicism, primitivism, serialism, electronic composition, modernism, post-modernism, minimalism, post-minimalism …

Neoclassicism: an anti-Romantic movement which took the clear and direct musical language of the eighteenth century and gave it a twentieth-century twang.

Twelve-tone music: a method of composition invented by Arnold Schoenberg which treats all twelve notes of the scale equally. Also known as serialism or dodecophany. Not to be confused with two-tone music, which is something else entirely.

Minimalism: invented in New York in the 1960s, a method of composition that uses hypnotically repeating patterns of notes which change gradually over time.

Sprechgesang: Also invented by Arnold Schoenberg, a vocal technique that blends speaking and singing.

Sampler: an instrument which records sounds in order for them to be manipulated and played back as part of a musical composition. Nothing to do with needlework – that's a different kind of sampler.